GOD'S FOOTPRINT IN BUSINESS

Bringing Transformation to the Marketplace

by

Alistair Petrie

Releasing The Kingdom of Heaven Series

CHI
BOOKS

WHAT OTHERS ARE SAYING ABOUT THIS BOOK ...

There is a secret caste system in the Church that suggests ministry is a "higher calling" than business. This is simply bad theology. Alistair Petrie, in his short but powerful book, *God's Footprint In Business*, constructs a compelling case for the ministry of business. We are all called to be disciples who are disciple-makers, and each of us, with our own unique talent-set, contributes to building the Kingdom of God, each of us being equal in value to God because we are doing His work. Petrie's case for Kingdom business finds that we are at our best when we work together, in harmony, with complementary skills ... and God is glorified in our work. Don't miss this excellent treatise on this timely subject.

Mark L. Maxwell
President – Prairie College, Three Hills, AB, Canada

My husband Mike and I have known Alistair for over 15 years. His unique understanding of the past, informed insight on the present, give him the unique ability to see future trends, helping others to skillfully navigate in an uncertain world. With his wise counsel and the help of a great team, I have experienced a high level of business success.

Debbie Bolton
Co-Founder & Global Chief Sales Officer – Norwex, Coppell, Texas, USA

In *God's Footprint In Business*, Alistair Petrie has given us a glimpse into the importance of the spiritual realm of business, and its role for success in our work life calling. Alistair brings valuable insights into understanding the unique relationship between generational sins and any open doors that could hinder success in our work – life call. I highly recommend this book for every serious follower of Christ who wants to operate in a Kingdom marketplace call.

Os Hillman
President – Marketplace Leaders Cumming, USA; Author – Today God Is First

Good road map of best practices for a Kingdom Business. A brilliant and concise guide for business to know, love and serve Jesus in the marketplace.

Greg Simpson
President & CEO – Simpson Seeds Inc., Saskatchewan, Canada's Best Managed Companies

I have had the pleasure of being a student of Alistair's work for a few years now and it is a book like this which explains so easily why. In a few short chapters he succinctly captures every key thing a Christian business person needs to understand, and take seriously, if they are to lead a truly Kingdom business. If you are a Christian in business, you NEED to read this!

Bobby Aitken
Managing Director – Momentum Improvement Partners, Perth, Australia

Alistair displays significant insights into the spiritual realities of God's Kingdom in the business realm. He describes with insight the fact that our actions, our unction, our obedience and our alliances significantly affect the spiritual and financial outcomes of our Christian business ventures and the Lord's willingness to come alongside with blessing and protection.

Robert Lundgren
President – Joshua Ministries Canada
Former Corporate Executive
Vancouver, Canada

Impacting! Revelatory! Compelling!

God's Footprint In Business is a ground–breaking book for Christians involved in business. Today there is much talk about digital transformation, but what is needed is spiritual transformation. Not only is this book sound theologically, it comes from many years of experience at ground level with communities and businesses throughout the world. Alistair has distilled what he has gathered and learned, and provided key insights and practical steps for application, challenging Christians in the marketplace to bring holiness into every facet of their business.

Is it possible to fathom the impact that a business can have on a community, city or nation, when that business is truly under the rule and reign of God? This book answers that question and is a foundational text for every Christian involved in business.

David and Margaret O'Connor
O'Connors Strata & Property Specialists, Parramatta, Australia

BY THE SAME AUTHOR

GOD'S DESIGN FOR CHALLENGING TIMES
Discovering Freedom in an Age of Compromise

IN HOLY FEAR
Rediscovering the Fear of the Lord

PROPHETIC DITCH DIGGING
Preparing For Breakthrough

Above CHI-Books titles available worldwide from online suppliers including:
www.amazon.com | www.koorong.com | www.bookdepository.co.uk | www.partnershipministries.org

eBooks available from: Amazon Kindle | Apple iBookstore | Barnes & Noble | Chapters | Koorong.com

TRANSFORMED! PEOPLES – CITIES – NATIONS
10 Principles for Sustaining Genuine Revival

Sovereign World Ltd, Lancaster, 2003: Republished 2008, Sovereign World Ltd

RELEASING HEAVEN ON EARTH

Grand Rapids, MI: Chosen Books, 2000: Republished 2008, Sovereign World Ltd

CHI–Books,
PO Box 6462, Upper Mt Gravatt,
Brisbane, QLD 4122, Australia

www.chibooks.org
publisher@chibooks.org

God's Footprint In Business – *Bringing Transformation to the Marketplace*
Copyright © 2019 by Rev. Dr Alistair Petrie

Print ISBN: 978-0-6480116-7-5
eBook ISBN: 978-0-6480116-8-2

Unless otherwise indicated, all Scripture quotations are taken from the HOLY BIBLE, NEW INTERNATIONAL VERSION®. NIV®. Copyright © 1973, 1978, 1984, 2011 by Biblica, Inc. ® Used by permission. All rights reserved worldwide.

Scripture quotations marked NASB are taken from the New American Standard Bible®, Copyright © 1960, 1962, 1963, 1968, 1971, 1972, 1973, 1975, 1977, 1995 by The Lockman Foundation. Used by permission (www.Lockman.org).

Printed in Australia, United Kingdom and the United States of America.

Distributed in the USA and internationally by Ingram Book Group and Amazon. Also available from: Bookdepository.co.uk and other outlets like Koorong.com in Australia.

Distribution of eBook version: Amazon Kindle, Apple iBooks, Koorong. com and others like Barnes & Noble NOOK, Sony eReader and KOBO.

Editorial assistance: Anne Hamilton
Cover design: Dave Stone
Layout: Jonathan Gould

ABOUT THE SERIES

In spite of the challenges we face in this day and age, we are also witnessing a move of God on an unprecedented global scale. This book is the second in a series that will enable us to connect to this worldwide move of God in the area of business and the marketplace. In the overall series we will illustrate specific and targeted types of prayer from Scripture as well as missional activity that will give us tools for breakthrough and change. As we will see in the pages that follow, this includes the world of business and the marketplace!

Over many decades of involvement in prayer and on-the-ground initiatives with leaders and communities within the global arena, we have repeatedly found the main challenge to be frustration, despair and not knowing how to obtain breakthroughs in seemingly impossible situations.

You will discover in this series wisdom and insight into a number of thrilling forms of prayer strategy God has given to His church. These are strategies that underline the promise of Luke 1:37 that indeed, nothing is impossible with God!

First book in the series: *Prophetic Ditch Digging—Preparing For Breakthrough.*

CONTENTS

INTRODUCTION

Marketplace—The Place Where Business is Done

This book is about releasing the Kingdom of God into the Marketplace—but not in the way you may expect. It is not a book about expertise in how to do the normal pragmatics of business—and increasing productivity—though that may well occur. It is a book that sees business through the lens of the Kingdom of God releasing Godly foundations in society. It is a book that explains how to transform our communities and cities through individual businesses—and seeing business as ministry, and ministry as business. The two go hand in hand and should never be separate.

CHAPTER 1
Business is Ministry

A Chiropractor and a Mayor

A chiropractor had attended one of our marketplace schools and heard that God can use any sphere of business as a tool for evangelism and transformation in a city. He returned home and went to meet with the Mayor to encourage him in making a formal declaration over the city. The Mayor took the challenge and wrote a proclamation saying the city belonged to the Lord! The proclamation was met with stiff opposition especially from groups not sympathetic with the Gospel. But the chiropractor, the mayor and their support group did not back down and withstood the resistance until it disappeared.

Time has passed, and the city is now experiencing economic growth even in the midst of a financial downturn. Religious traditions have become secondary to a genuine love for the Lord with an unconditional love for each other. Regional prejudice has been disappearing. The key has been walking and working in integrity and in holy fear before the Lord, which is a key for authentic community transformation (as explained in our book *In Holy Fear* [1]). The spiritual climate continues to change, and there

> From God's perspective work is actually part of worship.

is expectancy for a fully-fledged Revival in their city—but it took a Chiropractor with a vision and a Mayor with determination to start the momentum. They are examples of catalysts of change that God is raising up in the marketplace to release the culture of the Kingdom of God in cities and nations throughout the world in a time of profound global change.

A Biblical Foundation

Ministry in the Marketplace is not a new concept. It is the foundation for "hands on" ministry found in Scripture. In the New Testament, Jesus appeared in public 132 times of which 122 were in the marketplace. He teaches Kingdom principles in 52 Parables of which 45 have a workplace/marketplace context. He spent the majority of His adult life as a carpenter and regularly taught in a workplace environment, using everyday workplace examples.

Similarly, much of Paul's teaching was in the marketplace setting (see Acts 17:17).

Work and Worship

In the Old Testament, work and worship come from the same root Hebrew word *avodah*. From God's perspective work is actually part of worship, as long as we do not worship the work we do! In Psalm 90:17 we read: *"May the favor of the Lord our God rest on us; establish the work of our hands for us..."*

The fall of man resulted in a separation between God and His people resulting in the land being cursed—the very land God had called His people to steward. The redemption of the land involves bringing that land back under God's covenantal protection and blessing, and removing whatever has occurred in that place contrary to His purpose. This means understanding land from God's perspective and our call as His stewards over His property. Psalm 24:1 confirms His ownership of all land: *"The earth is the Lord's, and everything in it, the world, and all who live in it."*

The Psalmist shares a profound truth: *"Those the Lord blesses will inherit the land, but those He curses will be cut off "* (Psalm 37:22). This is important to grasp since it underlines an earlier principle God made concerning the subject of land:

> *"The land must not be sold permanently, because the land is Mine and you reside in My land as foreigners and strangers. Throughout the land that you hold as a possession, you must provide for the redemption of the land."* (Leviticus 25:23–24)

Land is a Key
Scripture refers to "land" 1717 times and contains the product of blessing and curse from previous years and generations. As explained more fully in our earlier book *Releasing Heaven on Earth*[2]*,* land is like a "feeding trough" for whatever takes place on that area—whether it is a church, a place of business, a community, a city, and even an entire nation. It affects both present and future generations. Unless we recalibrate our worldview to understand how the spiritual realm affects the physical realm, we may well be captive to significant limitations in any area of productivity and breakthrough we look for in our areas of responsibility.

Unaddressed issues allow a spiritual malaise to linger, limiting our breakthrough and keeping the thinking and the mindset of people in that area blind to the purposes of God (see 2 Corinthians 4:4). This, in turn, minimizes how they may respond to God's vision for them and their potential fruitfulness in that place. Understanding land is a key to our revelation.

All Business is Conducted on Land

Deuteronomy 8:18 refers to an amazing promise God has given to those who understand this issue of land and who hold to His covenant in their lives:

> "But remember the Lord your God, for it is He who gives you the ability to produce wealth, and so confirms His covenant, which He swore to your ancestors, as it is today."

However, a sobering reminder follows this promise:

> "If you ever forget the Lord your God and follow other gods and worship and bow down to them, I testify against you today that you will surely be destroyed. Like the nations the Lord destroyed before you, so you will be destroyed for not obeying the Lord your God." (Deuteronomy 8:19–20)

Being given the ability to produce refers to our ability to create, invent, secure, generate and steward God's wealth. He owns everything! But the sobering reminder is that this can be removed instantly if the intent of the heart is not pure—if we're not focused solely on the Lord. Both the Old and New Testaments remind us that **we reap what we sow** (see Proverbs 11:24–25,22:8–9; 2 Corinthians 9:6–11; Galatians 6:6–8)—and that we reap what others have sown before us—both bad and good!

The key principle is this—all business is conducted on land—including offices that regulate shipping and airline productivity. On land—on sea—or in the air—all business can be affected by the spiritual issues influencing the land and therefore the production of every type of commodity.

How then, can our occupations affect the work of the Kingdom of God? How can we address issues that affect our productivity?

CHAPTER 2
Entering the Marketplace

A Farm Becomes a Kingdom Template

A farmer contacted us on one occasion and asked if we would pray over his property (thousands of acres!) since the productivity of harvest on his land was not good. He had already spent considerable money in locating a well for his future home, but it turned out to be dry. Out of desperation he then called a friend who was known for his ability in finding sources of water. However, they sought water through the process of water witching – an occultic practice referred to in Scripture as 'divining', sometimes used "innocently" by people. As a Christian he repented of the practice and then we prayed for the land to be cleansed and healed. Within that harvest year, his productivity more than doubled and his grain export business began to increase exponentially. He, in turn, has been a key leader in his city, influencing other leaders in many streams of business to release the culture of the Kingdom of God in the city – one that is now well on its journey towards Community Transformation.

The Aroma of Christ

2 Corinthians 2:15–17 holds a key:

> *"For we are to God the aroma of Christ among those who are being saved and those who are perishing. To the one we are an aroma that brings death; to the other, an aroma that brings life… in Christ we speak before God with sincerity, as those sent from God."*

We know this to be true for our personal lives, but are we aware that this is also true concerning the "work of our hands"?

Paul clarifies this in Colossians 3:23–24: *"Whatever you do, work at it with all your heart, as working for the Lord, not for human masters, since you know that you will receive an inheritance from the Lord as a reward. It is the Lord Christ you are serving."* This is a principle for our personal lives, and especially so when we are in the world of business!

> Both the marketplace and synagogue were part of Paul's mandate for ministry.

In Acts 13 we learn that **Paul** (who was a tent maker) and **Barnabas** are sent out by Apostolic headquarters into the Marketplace (see Acts 13:2–3). Acts 18:2–3 records their meeting **Aquila and Priscilla**—both tentmakers. Paul stayed and *worked with them* (emphasis mine). In Acts 18:8, **Crispus**—who is the synagogue ruler—and his family are converted, as were many other people in Corinth. Paul remained there for 18 months (see Acts 18:11). Then Aquila and Priscilla led **Apollos**, known as a learned man, to faith (see Acts 18:24–26).

The list of Early Church professions that influenced all of society covered many arenas. **Lydia** was a wealthy wholesaler of expensive fabric. **Dorcas** was in design and manufacturing of inner garments (see Acts 9:39). **Erastus** was a city treasurer (see Romans 16:23). **Theophilus** was a government official (see Acts 1:1).

Acts 6 refers to the first **Deacons** who were proven businessmen of character and who could demonstrate and address faulty systems in society. These and many others did not simply fund the Apostles and church workers—they were the church influencing society from within the marketplace! Little wonder that the vast majority of miracles in the early years of the New Testament took place in the Marketplace, and not in the Synagogue!

Acts 19:10 states that all the Jews and Greeks who lived in Asia heard the Word of the Lord while Paul and his disciples stayed there for two years. Both the marketplace and synagogue were part of Paul's mandate for ministry. There was no distinct separation as is the case today in much of Western society.

Cleansing Foundations
A key shift occurs in Acts 19:20 when Paul visited Ephesus. During his time there the burning of occultic articles took place as the fear of the Lord gripped both Jews and Greeks (Acts 19:19). This resulted in a powerful spread of the Gospel (Acts 19:20). Here is a key template principle—when cleansing takes place within the area of our lives and businesses, there will be a cause-and-effect in both the spiritual and physical realms. Then the eyes and hearts of the people in the area are opened. However, if we are going to be people of influence for the Kingdom of God then this principle begins with us:

> "In a large house there are articles not only of gold and silver, but also of wood and clay; some for special purposes and some for common use. Those who cleanse themselves from the latter will be instruments for special purposes, made holy, useful to the Master and prepared to do any good work." (2 Timothy 2:20–21)

Accessing A City

Almost every community will have professions that are key for the life and work in that area. We refer to these professions as "access points"—these are areas of influence based on the specific nature of the professions. Described in detail in our book *God's Design For Challenging Times*[3], these areas of influence include:

> The Church and Religious Institutions
> The Political
> The Legal
> The Educational
> The Area of Industry, Trade and Commerce
> The Medical
> The Public Media
> Recreation and Sports
> The Armed Forces (if in that area).

While there may be several others, we generally find these areas cover most communities, cities and regions. These commodities influence the development and life and fruitfulness of each community—whether small or large. Each city—each business—is composed of vision, tradition, stewardship, culture, sociology and spirituality, which influence those who live and work there. Furthermore, every city and business is shaped by these components which continue to shape and affect those who are building upon earlier foundations.

Having a Firm Foundation

In 1 Corinthians 3:10-15, Paul issues a sober warning: *"...I laid a foundation as a wise builder, and someone else is building on it. But each one should build with care. For no one can lay any foundation other than the one already laid, which is Jesus Christ... their work will be shown for what it is... It will be revealed with fire, and the fire will test the quality of each person's work..."*

What is significant in this passage is that Paul is using the word "foundation" for building, which is the same word used in the foundation of human personality and character.

Psalm 127:1 sounds a salient warning for anything we build: *"Unless the LORD builds the house, They labor in vain who build it; Unless the LORD guards the city, The watchman keeps awake in vain"* (NASB). This means we need to ensure each part of the building and development has a solid foundation reflecting the Kingdom of God if we want to be assured of His reign and rule in our lives. A city, or business, takes on the foundation and personality of those who influence its development.

A Storage Facility Becomes a Kingdom Template

Business owners of a large storage facility approached us and asked if we would come and pray over their property. They had developed this facility as a form of income but also as a means of utilizing profit for funding mission projects. However, the facility was far from full which meant their costs were marginalizing any profit from the business. Upon undertaking research as part of the prayer project, it was found that the early foundations of the property were influenced by early forms of tribal warfare and bloodshed. Later this was compounded with fear and trauma in the lives of young armed forces personnel who were trained there in preparation for overseas warfare. Furthermore, there was a history of death on this land.

The current business owners had legal right to the land and in keeping with Leviticus 25:23–24 and 2 Chronicles 7:14–16, we joined them in identificational prayer and began the process of cleansing the foundations of all that had been unholy in God's sight. This had given the demonic the right of access to that area (see Ephesians 4:27) and had caused barrenness instead of fruitfulness. We explain in detail what cleansing the land involves in our books *In Holy Fear*[4] and *Releasing Heaven On Earth*.[5]

Within weeks the change was profound and not only was the storage facility full, but there was also a waiting list for others wanting to store their items there. When asked why they wanted this particular storage facility (and not one closer to home where some of these people lived), their response indicated that they felt this particular place felt "safe". There was a sense of peace and rest here, and this is where they wanted to store their belongings! Since that day, this storage facility has been a marketplace template of Kingdom ministry influencing the area.

CHAPTER 3
Spiritual Foundations in the Marketplace

God has a love for our community—but He may not love whatever is taking place there! As we have now seen, His presence requires holiness both in the lives of people as well as in the work of their hands.

The challenge for many people active in the present-day Marketplace is to think *spirituallly* while living and working *pragmatically*. Western-based education does not readily teach the spiritual issues when dealing with bricks and mortar! And yet, as we saw in Acts 19:20, the removal of unholy objects shifted the atmosphere resulting in the extension of the Gospel. Our **worldview** needs to see reality through the lens of the Holy Spirit, otherwise mindsets and productivity for the Kingdom of God in any area will be significantly limited.

Uncover—Discover—Recover
On one occasion we were asked to participate in praying through a privately-owned pharmaceutical company. The owner was a Christian and he knew something was wrong, but no remedy could be found. The company was coming to a halt.

> Our worldview needs to see reality through the lens of the Holy Spirit.

A combination of prayer, research and direct questioning revealed that, on the day the computer system stopped, the owner had hired a new computer programmer. This man, upon entering the computer department, had hung a raw chicken upside down over the operation systems. His religious affiliation saw the importance of bringing an offering to the god he served in order for his work to be done effectively. Instead it brought an immediate unholiness into the life and productivity of this Kingdom company and all operations seized! There was a conflict of two kingdoms at work. Everything returned to normal once the owner repented of permitting this type of occultic offering to have occurred.

We have learned over the years that when we ask the right questions, God will provide the answer. In other words, *why* are things the way they are—*how* and *when* did the issues begin—and then *what* can be done to address the situation. Or, putting it another way...

God wants us to **UNCOVER** the problems.
But he asks us to **DISCOVER** what has occurred.
Then He will enable us to **RECOVER** His Kingdom purposes.

We are reminded in 2 Chronicles 29:5–7, 16–17 that idols of any kind can defile a place, but what has been defiled can be made holy again (see 2 Chronicles 29:3–17). It is the sinful activities or beliefs of the people—whether past or present—that affect both land and whatever is built upon the land. Under the New Covenant, the Law still remains but the solution for breaking the Law is different (see Leviticus 18:24–25; 20:22–24; Matthew 5:17–18). Occult practices include everything contrary to the character of God (see Deuteronomy 18:9–13) and render a person — a church — a building — a city — even a nation — vulnerable to the influence of the demonic.

It is the sinful beliefs and activities of past and present occupants and owners that give the enemy the right of access (see Ephesians 4:27; Revelation 12:10). Once there is any form of spiritual access, it remains until the original issue is addressed through confession and repentance. When lack of productivity and being unable to sustain any form of breakthrough for the Kingdom of God persists, it is time to review the spiritual foundations in order to understand what is happening physically.

A Spiritual Checklist for your Business
Over the years we have developed a spiritual checklist for Kingdom business that enables people in the marketplace to ask the necessary questions in order to seek the correct solutions:

- ◊ Is there a substantial employee turnover?
- ◊ What is the overall feeling about job satisfaction?
- ◊ Do your employees reflect high or low self-esteem?
- ◊ Is there any bickering, back-biting, or jealousy within the organization?
- ◊ Is there any internal theft?
- ◊ How is the productivity?
- ◊ How is the profit margin—are finances up or down?
- ◊ Are employees jockeying for position?
- ◊ Is there any evidence of occultic activity?
- ◊ Is absenteeism normal or increasing?
- ◊ Have there been any cases of sexual abuse?
- ◊ Are trade union issues more problematic than usual?
- ◊ Is there any confusion between leadership or management —especially in terms of decision-making?
- ◊ Has a potential hostile takeover ever been an issue?

◊ Has anything changed since the last partner or board member came on board? If so, in what way?

◊ Has there ever been any history of "clandestine" funding—where the source may be questionable?

We can be a Christian in business—without understanding why any of the above occurs. In other words, there is a difference between being a Christian in business in contrast to a Christian who seeks the rule and reign of the culture of the Kingdom of God in his or her area of responsibility. The latter requires doing business from a totally different perspective.

> The power of repentant prayer changes people and cities.

A City is Changed

In Acts 8:5–8 we read of a city in Samaria that has been influenced by the occult, but which changed to a city full of joy following the ministry of Philip. In other words, the city experienced deliverance!

In 2 Chronicles 29, Hezekiah inherits a godless land due to the sin of his fathers. The context tells us of complete spiritual and physical barrenness due to the sin of the leadership, including the priests! Following the necessary cleansing of the leaders—including the city officials (members of the marketplace—see 2 Chronicles 29:20)—major shift came to the entire land and we are told that Hezekiah and all the people rejoiced at what God had done so quickly for His people. The power of repentant prayer changes people and cities—and the businesses within those cities.

> Proverbs 11:10–11 reminds of this important principle: *"When the righteous prosper, the city rejoices... Through the blessing of the upright a city is exalted..."*

We all have an assigned sphere of influence and it is important to understand the importance of praying within our areas of responsibility, no matter what our area of work may involve. Paul warns us about this in 2 Corinthians 10:13–17:

> *"We, however, will not boast beyond proper limits, but will confine our boasting to the sphere of service God Himself has assigned to us, a sphere that also includes you... For we do not want to boast about work already done in someone else's territory..."*

The Psalmist refers to our places of responsibility (boundary lines) since these become *"pleasant places"* and a *"delightful inheritance"* (see Psalm 16:6). The Lord wants us to enter the fullness of our inheritance at all levels of life—including our productivity (see Psalm 78:55).

God promises His healing in our lives and in the work of our hands—which involves redeeming the land He has given us (see Leviticus 25:23–24). In Leviticus 26 we learn of the breakthroughs that come from our obedience to this mandate which are the benefits God wants us to experience: [6]

Ecological Health (Leviticus 26:4)
Economic Health (Leviticus 26:5)
Personal Security (Leviticus 26:6a)
Civil Security (Leviticus 26:6b)
International Security (Leviticus 26:7-8a)
Honor and Growth (Leviticus 26:9)
Innovation and Creativity (Leviticus 26:10)

As a ministry—we have witnessed all of the above occurring at different levels in a complete variety of marketplace settings once the owners and stewards in these areas make a choice for a Kingdom business.

But first, the foundations of each commodity had to be examined.

CHAPTER 4
Knowing Our Foundations

Non-Negotiable Kingdom Principles
There are essential Kingdom principles we need to understand if we are to differentiate between a business run by Christians in contrast to being involved in a Kingdom business. A Kingdom ministry/business understands the original root and core level rationale for its existence—it exists to extend the Kingdom of God in society! Will the business truly bring honor and glory to the Lord?

If the land has unaddressed spiritual issues, it will affect the people and the productivity of the business. Similarly, if the people at any level of activity are not living and working in a posture of holiness, then this, in turn, will affect the land and infrastructure of the business.

Original Grass Roots
We need to be aware of the thinking and intent of the original grass roots in the founding leadership. What about the present leadership? What about the shareholders? When the latter are asked to become part of a Christian enterprise, their

> If there is questionable fruit in the productivity of the company, always check the roots!

heart motivation has huge implications in the on-going direction and productivity of the enterprise.

Root and Fruit Issues

We have found that faulty or unholy roots will ultimately have a detrimental effect upon the fruit (productivity). As we saw in chapter 1, the non-negotiable principle in Scripture is that we always reap what has been sown. This inevitably influences the growth and development of the company and either releases strength for on-going growth or minimizes effectiveness—especially if we are looking at becoming a Kingdom business. Little wonder both secular and Christian-based companies are being exposed today due to the results of earlier cover-up, witting or unwitting, of "unholy seed-sowing".

The working principle is simple and straightforward—if there is **questionable fruit** in the productivity of the company, **always check the roots**! In one Kingdom business we have worked with that has grown substantially over the years, there came a point in which the cover-up on the part of one key employee was exposed simply because the "fruit" in the productivity had caused key clients to disengage from the company. This, in turn, prompted the CEO to undertake an investigation. He discovered that this key employee had been conducting highly improper business practices and had sown "unholiness" into the entire company.

The result was large financial loss. The CEO repented for not having had greater care in ensuring his employee had been conducting business properly. It required his making restitution to certain clients in order for the company to regain its momentum. A costly lesson—but essential in terms of how this company is now engaging the global market.

Honesty and Integrity

Is there honesty and integrity in what is being said and done? Does this include all advertising—all levels of productivity? Can the Ananias and Sapphira issue be avoided? (see Acts 5:1–11). It has been said that God is not just a lip-reader—He reads the thoughts and intentions of the heart. We therefore need to clarify the values and methodology of the "product". Is this for the Lord, or is it for the existence of the company itself and its shareholders?

Board of Directors/Elders

What are their present "heart" issues? What else occurs in their "life portfolio"? Why did they become part of the organization? Was it out of expediency? Was it due to their skills? Or did it "look good" to bring them on board? This is important to grasp since their influence will have a significant cause-and-effect in what happens in the organization. If they bring a questionable "far country" (soul ties/motivation) to the table, this affects fruitfulness and decision-making.

Founder's Spirit-Syndrome

The vision of a founder can affect an organization in crucial ways. Even a "**familiar spirit**" from one of the early founders can latch on to the present generation and be transferred on to future generations. To prevent this, the present-day stewards (you and me) should address whatever is contrary to God's vision.

One mission organization asked for our help in addressing continual financial issues which always occurred at a crucial moment of breakthrough. Only when we researched the original founder's belief that the ministry would never expand beyond a certain level was it understood that a **limitation** had been placed upon all the future productivity of this ministry. He was a Godly man but nevertheless he had limited what God could do through false humility and reduced expectancy. The present Director repented of this false belief in God's capability. Within weeks (and to this day), the ministry expanded well beyond any previous limit—since now its mandate rested solely upon the God of the impossible.

Unholy Alliances

Alliances can be both witting and unwitting—as well as being both helpful and unhelpful.

Our "far country" refers to everything present in our lives both previous and current—the strengths and the weaknesses, the positives and the negatives. When we enter the covenant of marriage, we bring who we are into the relationship. However we also bring in unseen and often unknown elements—these pertain to events that happened in the generations before us and include characteristics both in the spiritual and physical realms. Only when the marriage covenant is ratified do we begin to learn what else may have entered the marriage—and that may now need to be addressed!

The same principle applies in our areas of work. Who we are and what we do and what we carry with us affects the organization. This is why we require diligent prayers in each part of a Kingdom company in order that nothing remains joined to—attached to—or is in covenant with—any part of the organization that is contrary to the purposes of God. Otherwise it will have a negative cause and effect upon the operation of the entire company— such as we saw earlier in the case of the pharmaceutical firm.

Third party venture partners have a "spiritual portfolio" that become part of the "one flesh" that affects and influences the overall "DNA" of any organization. This opens up the whole area of "spiritual soul ties" and possible spiritual co-dependency.

When new partners are asked to join a company, or when a third party is asked to invest financially, the money that is part of the agreement also represents whatever spiritual values may be attached to that person and whatever hidden agendas may be part of the overall package!

Spiritual twinning can result in significant ramifications to any organization when any "far country" is transferred or imported into the organization with permission coming from the leadership. While such an investment/transfer can be positive—if it is not of God, it can also be lethal. While such a transfer or investment of funds can be cleansed of anything contrary to God's purposes, this becomes subject to the Lord's direction. At times He clearly does not want a certain investment or agreement to be made, as it will give later leverage to the enemy to have the right of access to the productivity of that organization.

Spiritual twinning of communities and cities is often encouraged these days, and while such agreements made between at-home and overseas cities can be helpful in terms of politics and trade and tourism, there are unseen spiritual agreements also being made that can affect one city through the spiritual culture of another—such as we have seen on many occasions. Again, **this will challenge our worldview** if we are not thinking spiritually!

Watch Out For Those "Gifts"!
One city in North America we are personally familiar with intentionally entered into a relational covenant with a city in Japan which, in turn, sent a set of Shinto gates to this city as a gift and seal of relationship. The Gates were duly positioned outside the entrance to the city. Within months the strengths of this small city began to weaken—its trade and commerce faltered, its tourism waned, the church unity began to dissolve, and the local intercessors sensed great unrest and division enter the city.

When we met with them at their request it was clear that the Lord was saying the city had intentionally changed its allegiance to worshipping another spirit. Decisions made by the few in areas of authority, affected the city as a whole, and "unseen" spiritual soul ties with the overseas city had negatively affected almost every area of life. Through prayer and repentance, these issues were addressed resulting in positive changes to trade and commerce and tourism. Later, other Christian marketplace leaders continued to pray and bring further correction resulting in significant change and growth in that city—numerically, economically, and spiritually.

Spiritual Soul Ties in Business

Rarely would this topic ever be taught in schools of commerce or business administration. Pragmatically, it makes no sense. But in the spirit realm it makes all the sense in the world since a "spirit" can gain access into whatever we do, own, agree upon— and receive. It is the unseen element in relationships—but which can significantly affect all parties involved.

Matthew 11:29 refers to a holy soul tie when we are yoked to the Lord, whereas Paul warns us in 2 Corinthians 6:14–17 to be cautious of being yoked with unbelievers. He states in verse 14: *"What do righteousness and wickedness have in common"*? A succinct warning! But then he states:

> *"What does a believer have in common with an unbeliever? What agreement is there between the temple of God and idols? For we are the temple of the living God. As God has said: 'I will live with them and walk among them, and I will be their God, and they will be my people.' Therefore, 'Come out from them and be separate, says the Lord. Touch no unclean thing and I will receive you.'"* (2 Corinthians 6:16–17)

Scripture views this subject of soul ties and being yoked to others seriously since there is substantial warning in both the

Old and New Testaments.[7] It has huge impact upon the world of business. Put simply, our soul (mind, will, intellect, imagination) joins our spiritual to our physical. The soul was designed to be governed by the Spirit of God in relationship to the human spirit. Therefore, it becomes a spiritual bond with anyone related to it through sex — generation — covenant — money — holding godly cords of love or ungodly cords of captivity and bondage.

The Ships Are Sunk!

Jehoshaphat learned this lesson the hard way. In 2 Chronicles 20:35–37 a sobering lesson unfolds for this king. He has just experienced an amazing victory over his enemies thanks to the unique strategy and intervention of the Lord (see 2 Chronicles 20:1–29). But he seemingly forgets what the Lord has just taught him and enters into an alliance (soul tie) with Ahaziah, a wicked king of Israel. They entered into a business partnership involving the building of a fleet of trading ships, but then we read these sobering words spoken by a prophet who understood the detrimental nature of this soul tie: *"'Because you have made an alliance with Ahaziah, the Lord will destroy what you have made.' The ships were wrecked and were not able to set sail to trade."* (2 Chronicles 20:37)

> Marketplace ministry is a non-negotiable catalyst of redemption if we truly want to see authentic transformation.

Unholy Influence

2 John verse 11 explains that when we partner with business associates who are ungodly in their lives and/or in their way of doing business, we actually come under their influence: *"Anyone who welcomes them shares in their wicked work."* This means

we partner, or are yoked, in his evil work—which is exactly why a Kingdom business will have problems if connections and agreements and partnerships are formed that bring unholy decision-making or lifestyles into the organization.

As Paul states in 1 Corinthians 6:16 when we have sex with a prostitute we are uniting ourselves as one flesh. Graphic words! Entering into unholy agreements has the same spiritual impact as having sex with a prostitute. That is a very clear warning! He does not want His holiness in our lives to be shared with any form of unholiness—and this includes Kingdom business. Instead He wants us cut free from the cords of the wicked (see Psalm 129:4).

Marketplace ministry is a non-negotiable catalyst of redemption if we truly want to see authentic transformation and destiny released in cities and nations before the return of the Lord. Even as a business, those who comprise that enterprise can enter into the ministry of confession and forgiveness, repentance, spiritual warfare, and healing. This is part of ministry in the marketplace! As seen earlier, we are to work within our spheres of influence (see 2 Corinthians 10:13–15) and our boundary lines of responsibility (see Psalm 16:5–6). In so doing both individuals and churches, as well as Kingdom templates within the marketplace, become God's instruments for releasing His transforming power in society.

CHAPTER 5
Business—Traditional or Kingdom?

We have learned that God owns the land and it is always His land no matter what is built and developed upon it. Our responsibility is to possess the land. This means to seek its redemption (see Leviticus 25:23–24) and to steward the results/blessings as outlined in Leviticus 26:3–13.

Are We Owners or Tenants?

Even though Leviticus 25 and Psalm 24 state God owns all the land on the earth, as His stewards we are given a unique calling. However, we are not to have a 'tenant mentality'—one that has little sense of responsibility to the land. A tenant pays a rent, but often has little concern for the upkeep and appearance and general well-being of the property. God owns the land but bequeaths to us the responsibility of looking after His property **as if it were our own,** and allows us to reap the productivity and benefits from the land.

Profit and Leverage for the Kingdom

Therefore, we are called to bring about a yield and harvest that honours the One who has called us to be responsible for it on His terms. This principle lies at the heart of many of the stewardship parables in the New Testament. We are given the mandate to redeem what has been lost: *"For the Son of Man has come to seek and to save that which was lost."* (Luke 19:10 NASB)

What has been lost? If we condense this massive topic we find that due to the Fall, we lost intimacy, innocence, and an understanding of purity. We lost our communication with God and developed a gender division (man vs. woman) along with a generational division (Adam and Eve and Cain and Abel). We entered into the reality of death and the need of doing hard labour on the land. We lost His covering over us as citizens of God. We developed our human culture but lost the direction of the Lord in our lives (see 1 Corinthians 2). We forfeited an understanding of Godly marketplace ministry and so allowed unholy foundations to develop in society (see Genesis 4:17–27).

In Christ, this is all returned to us, along with His intimacy in our lives and a knowledge of His ways. This becomes a key foundational garment for all of society, especially within Marketplace ministry—which is part of the prophetic voice of God in society.

In the Parable of the Minas (Luke 19:11–27), we are given the mandate of responsibility which includes an investment of return on the investment. The order is important to note—and part of the responsibility includes a jurisdiction over cities (see Luke 19:17–19).

In the Parable of the Shrewd Manager (Luke 16:1–15) we learn that we are the managers of the owner's possessions. The Parable itself contains deep insight into God's expectation of us, but clearly states: *"I tell you, use worldly wealth to gain friends for yourselves, so that when it is gone, you will be welcomed into eternal dwellings. Whoever can be trusted with very little can also be trusted with much"* (Luke 16:9–10). But it continues saying we need to be trustworthy in handling worldly wealth before we can be trusted with true riches (see Luke 16:10–11).

The Parable of the Sower (Matthew 13) instructs us to address and remove the birds that eat the seeds, the shallow soil and the thorns on the land in order to be assured of a good harvest— whether a hundred, sixty, or thirty times what was sown. All this is our jurisdiction— and God has an expectancy that we will produce a harvest for the Kingdom. Not only that, God blesses proper stewardship with further responsibility (see Luke 12:48b).

Traditional vs. Kingdom Business

Now we can compare a **traditional business**—one that has limited understanding about the ownership and stewardship of land on God's terms—and compare it to a **God-owned and Kingdom-directed business**.

In a **traditional business** the primary purpose of the enterprise is to make a living and earn money, believing that the counsel of man holds all the equity.

> In a **Kingdom business** under the rule and reign of God, the main purpose is to bless the Lord, His people, and the nations, believing that God owns all the equity, and shares it with His people.

In a **traditional business** we retain assets to build personal net worth in which owners and shareholder can become wealthy with occasional tithing for worthwhile projects (though sometimes simply for taxation purposes).

> In a **Kingdom business** assets and ownership are normally seen as Kingdom holdings, with an encouragement towards generosity at all levels (see 2 Corinthians 8:8–15). The power and product of true giving comes from the heart.

In a **traditional business** there is more of an owner/employee mentality, often with a considerable salary disparity. The "CEO" can be seen as a king-type figure and someone to please and appease.

In a **Kingdom business** all are workers and tenants for God's enterprise, with varying roles and talents, seeing each gift set as necessary for building up the whole.

In a **traditional business** there can often be subtle competitiveness between the team members, highlighting another's weakness.

In a **Kingdom business**, there is a sense of completing each other in which one's strength covers another's weakness.

In a **traditional business** all levels of leadership and the investors will have mixed motivations and faith beliefs.

In a **Kingdom business** the key leaders and staff will have a passion for the Lord and have a desire to pray for and with each other and for the company.

In a **traditional business** a primary objective can be to position the company for eventual sale and profit from the increased value with an eventual sale to the highest bidder with little concern as to who that may be.

In a **Kingdom business**, there is genuine pastoral concern for all the company members and to extend it as a catalyst for Kingdom purposes.

In a **traditional business** there is normally very little impact for the Kingdom and there is a tendency to compromise to political sensitivity at the expense of the Gospel.

In a **Kingdom business** the company sees itself as part of the body of Christ seeking to advance the Kingdom of God on earth both locally and beyond.

Furthermore, in a **Kingdom business,** there is a desire to align with the purposes of God and develop a legacy that disciples, models, trains and prepares the next generation for leadership.

The Kingdom business sees itself as a *ministry* responding to whatever issues need to be addressed within society and one that reflects the Kingdom of God at all levels of life from the leadership to the client and from the raw material to the finished product.

This is the type of business that understands the **power of prayer** even in the midst of secular pragmatics.

CHAPTER 6
The Power of Marketplace Intercession

If we want a Kingdom culture within our place of business, then prayer with insight and understanding is essential. Either company intercessors and/or those we call alongside us will know what to be praying for, and also how to be praying "Thy Kingdom Come".

Informed Intercession
We start with an understanding of the times in which we live and being aware of the signs of these times and how we **respond** rather than **react** to what is going on around us. In other words, as a business we seek to learn to respond, and not to react, and to understand how our business relates to the times in which we live.

Praying Through the Issues
Either for people or for a company, the way we pray is similar. This involves confession and forgiveness, and the breaking of any mindsets and bondages that are contrary to the purposes of God for the company and for the area. We need to remember that a Kingdom business can be a catalyst of change for the

> If we want a Kingdom culture within our place of business, then prayer with insight and understanding is essential.

city. We have authority to pray through these issues through position of office or ownership.

Spiritual Diagnosis

To pray with understanding, we need to know how to research the area and to see what impediments and obstacles may be encountered. We are addressing whatever consequences of sin may have affected the land as a result of idolatry, immorality, untimely bloodshed, or broken covenant—any or all of which may have occurred in previous years or generations. We are not to build on an unholy foundation. In the case of a church, if previous congregations have been subject to splits and disunity, we need to find out why. In the case of business, if previous companies have folded or entered into bankruptcy, find out why and ensure there is no access or foothold on the land for that to occur again.

Removing Unholy Foundations

God has given us the authority to remove that which is contrary to His Kingdom within whatever sphere of influence or responsibility He has given us. Following the prayer pattern above, we remove what is unholy in His sight and restore foundations in our work and relationships that reflect the Kingdom of God.

A Trojan Horse

We seek to ensure there are no unholy alliances or soul ties that have entered the company through any of the team, past or present however good they might look on the surface. Beware of potential "Trojan Horses"!

On one occasion we were praying for a very large and profitable company whose owner displayed gifts received from leaders of other nations. Due to his **fear of man** he simply would not remove a specific unholy object in his "trophy cabinet" and in the end the entire company became subject to a hostile takeover—he mixed holiness with the profane, even though he had been warned of the consequences several times. When more is given to us, more responsibility is also expected from us! It is important to have occasional spiritual inventories of the goods and assets displayed within our company and see what needs to be improved—or removed!

The Fear of the Lord
Therefore, in light of this, we learn how to work in the **power of the opposite spirit** and to release the **Fear of the Lord** in society.[8] This is a mandate both for the individual and the church, but also for any representative part of the Body of Christ, including a Kingdom business!

Checklist for Prayer:
- ◊ Understanding God's timing in decision-making.
- ◊ Speaking His life into our business and that God's will is done on earth through the company, as it is done in heaven.
- ◊ Seeking on-going protection from the schemes of the enemy—especially since we can be susceptible to third party venture in business which may—or may not—be of God. We need wisdom to know the difference, and to recognize a wolf in sheep's clothing.
- ◊ Praying for God's favor with new clients, markets, and ideas. He is the God of Vision who pioneers and perfects and wants to finish what He has begun in our midst (see Hebrews 12:1–2).

◊ Praying for righteousness in all relationships between employees, clients and partners and in all business practices (avoiding compromise at all costs). This includes praying for a proper delegation of authority and not allowing authoritarianism to preside.

◊ Praying for a spirit of Godliness to permeate every aspect of the company. People will be drawn to Him through the aroma of Christ at work throughout the business.

◊ Regular prayer for all the leaders — their families — their health — their relationships — their finances — and keeping short accounts on issues that need to be addressed in order that the Enemy receives no footholds (see Ephesians 4:27) and has no right to accuse (see Revelation 12:10).

◊ Praying that all areas of vulnerability in any of the above are quickly brought to the surface and addressed.

◊ Praying that all of the above is regularly stewarded with the Guard — Keep — and Occupy principle in mind.[9]

◊ Ensuring that the Intercessors are also prayed for and that regular meetings between intercessors and key company personnel occur in order that the counsel of the Lord is kept active and healthy.

Conclusion

A Kingdom business is a matter of choice. While we can do business according to worldly standards, this rarely will have lasting Kingdom impact either in the business itself, or in a city. However, if we choose to have the rule and reign of God in our business, then it becomes *His* business governed by the standards of the Kingdom of God.

Marketplace ministry is not a new concept. God worked in Creation — Jesus worked doing His Father's business — the Early Church extended the Kingdom of God simply by being in the Marketplace. This has always been God's design. We all look forward to the day when we hear the Father saying: *"Well done, good and faithful servant!"* (Matthew 25:23)

Simply put, Business is Ministry and Ministry is Business!

ENDNOTES

1. *In Holy Fear*, Rev. Dr Alistair Petrie, CHI-Books, PO Box 6462, Upper Mount Gravatt, QLD 4122 Australia, ISBN 978-0-9942607-2-7

2. *Releasing Heaven on Earth*, Rev. Dr Alistair Petrie, Sovereign World Ltd, ISBN 978-1852404819. Now out of print but further teaching resources concerning this subject are available on our ministry website, www.partnershipministries.org

3. *God's Design For Challenging Times*, Rev. Dr Alistair Petrie, pages 107–110, CHI-Books, PO Box 6462, Upper Mount Gravatt, QLD 4122 Australia, ISBN 978-0-9870891-0-6

4. *In Holy Fear*, Rev. Dr Alistair Petrie, CHI-Books, pages 90–100, PO Box 6462, Upper Mount Gravatt, QLD 4122 Australia, ISBN 978-0-9942607-2-7

5. *Releasing Heaven on Earth*, Rev. Dr Alistair Petrie, Sovereign World Ltd, ISBN 978-1852404819. Now out of print but further teaching resources concerning this subject are available on our ministry website, www.partnershipministries.org

6. For a complete outline and description of healing the land, please refer to our website which offers teachings and resources: www.partnershipministries.org

7. For more information on the subject of soul ties, we recommend *Soul Ties – The Unseen Bond in Relationships*, David Cross, Sovereign World, PO Box 784, Ellel, Lancaster LA1 9DA, England ISBN 978-1-85240-451-2

8. *In Holy Fear*, Rev. Dr Alistair Petrie, CHI-Books, pages 90–100, PO Box 6462, Upper Mount Gravatt, QLD 4122 Australia, ISBN 978-0-9942607-2-7. In particular see chapters 3 and 4 (pages 49–71)

9. For a thorough teaching on the principles of stewarding the issues of transformation and genuine revival, see *Transformed! – People – Cities – Nations*, Rev. Dr Alistair Petrie, Sovereign World, PO Box 784, Ellel, Lancaster LA1 9DA, England ISBN 978-1-85240-482-6. Now out of print but is available on our ministry website, www.partnershipministries.org

ABOUT THE AUTHOR

Rev. Dr Alistair P. Petrie

For many years in both the United Kingdom and Canada, Alistair served as senior pastor in diverse city church settings. With that experience and his earlier years spent in professional broadcasting, he now serves as the Executive Director of Partnership Ministries, a global ministry that teaches the principles and relevance of the Gospel and its relationship to the wider Church, the Marketplace, to Cities and to Nations. Partnership Ministries is positioned as a ministry for the 21st Century Church and combines prayer and research to prepare for lasting revival, authentic transformation and the release of Kingdom culture. In doing so, Alistair consults regularly with churches and ministries, businesses, and business leaders helping them in applying the principles of Transformation in their areas of influence — and explains how this releases cities and nations into their respective destinies.

Alistair travels extensively to many nations researching and teaching these transformation principles, in both church and city settings as well as in the marketplace arena. Obtaining his Doctorate through Fuller Seminary, he has been a guest lecturer at several academic settings and Schools of Ministry. As well as being an international speaker, he is the author of several books, and along with his ministry team has produced an informative DVD teaching series. He is married to Marie and along with their two sons, Mike and Richard, their entire family serve the wider church and the Marketplace in the global arena.

For more information on Partnership Ministries regarding their tools, training resources and webinars, please visit their website.

www.partnershipministries.org

Lightning Source UK Ltd.
Milton Keynes UK
UKHW020914181122
412419UK00012B/142